The Magic of Neon

To Lynda, *lumen de lumine*

THE MAGIC OF NEON

MICHAEL WEBB

➔

Gibbs M. Smith, Inc.
Peregrine Smith Books
Salt Lake City
1984

Second printing, 1984

Copyright © 1983 by Gibbs M. Smith, Inc.
All rights reserved for all countries, including the right
of translation. No part of this book may be used or
reproduced without written permission from the
publisher.

Library of Congress Cataloging in Publication Data
Webb, Michael, 1937-
  The magic of neon,
  Bibliography: p.81
  1. Neon lamps. 2. Neon tubes. 1. Title.
TK4383.W4   1983   621.32'75   83-14532
ISBN 0-87905-140-X

Book design by J. Scott Knudsen

Printed and bound in Japan

Cover: original neon art work by © Lili Lakich.

Table of Contents

Acknowledgements

Many people made valuable contributions to this book. My special thanks to Olivia Georgia, Richard Koshalek, Lili Lakich, and Tod Swormstedt for their encouragement and helpful suggestions for the improvement of the manuscript, and to Gibbs M. Smith and Buckley C. Jeppson of Peregrine Smith Books.

I am also most grateful to David Ablon, Robert Abrams, Larry Albright, Stephen Antonakos, Charles di Bona, Ted Bonar, Vaughan M. Cannon, Jr., William Christenberry, Laddie John Dill, Tricia Everett, Rosamund Felsen, Dennis Gastner, Anthony Goldschmidt, Susan Grode, Sam Grogg, Mark Gulezian, Michael Hauenstein, Michael Hayden, Malcolm Holzman, Fiona Irving, Richard Jenkins, Larry Kanter, Arthur J. Krim, Sherry Lang, Michael Margulies, Norman McGrath, David Naylor, Mary Jane O'Donnell, Gloria Poore, Robert Rauschenberg, Brenda Richardson, Jerry Rife, Alejandro Sina, Tama Starr, Dennis Thomas, Jeff Walker, Tony Walton, Melinda Wortz, Virginia Wright, Thomas Young, Jr., and Eric Zimmerman.

Michael Webb
Los Angeles, 1983

Across the United States, neon is enjoying a dramatic renaissance. It took twenty years for neon (which was launched in Paris in 1910) to achieve wide popularity. So, too, the revival—which began with a handful of artists and designers in the early sixties—is now winning general acceptance.

Designers are using neon with growing assurance: in movies (*The Wiz, One from the Heart, Blade Runner,* and a host of space fantasies), on stage, and in television; to animate discos, and to create a romantic ambience in restaurants and domestic interiors. Artists have exploited its line, light, and color—by itself or in combination with other materials. Major museums have presented retrospectives; architects, corporations, and civic authorities have commissioned large neon sculptures to enliven public buildings and darkened streets. In 1981, the Washington Project for the Arts organized a big outdoor exhibition, *Neon Fronts,* in the heart of the capital.

A new generation of artisans has begun to revitalize the endangered craft of neon. Neon workshops, some offering instruction in design and fabrication, are flourishing nationwide. Preservation societies, collectors, and a recently established Museum of Neon Art in Los Angeles have rallied to restore the old and foster the new. Nostalgic affection for old signs—which recall a safer, more cheerful era in urban living—has prompted a commercial revival. Classics are being relit. Neon is being used to ornament trendy boutiques, outline facades, and accent billboards and window displays.

The rediscovery of neon's creative potential coincides with a shift in public taste. Post-modern architecture, the return of figurative painting, the inventive recycling of old buildings and neighborhoods demonstrate a craving for color and ornament, and the rejection of blandness and austerity. Flamboyant movie palaces that seemed as doomed as the dinosaur have been recognized as priceless treasures.

In the thirties, neon was regarded as the epitome of glamor and progress, and it rapidly achieved the status of a popular art form. Its heyday was brief. By the fifties it was beginning to lose ground, the victim of new lighting techniques, rising costs, and a general decline in the standards of craftsmanship. Vacuum-formed plastics and fluorescent tubes eroded the appeal of neon, just as television challenged the preeminence of the movies. It lingered on, concealed in plastic-fronted channel lettering, and in such standardized roles as beer signs and pedestrian crossings. Poor maintenance and a popular association with bars and strip joints further lowered its reputation.

Worse was to come. Civic do-gooders and teenage vandals were equally destructive. Glass benders retired and were not replaced. Large signs were extinguished in response to the energy crises of the seventies—even though neon consumes only a fraction of the power of incandescent lighting.

Yet neon has proved surprisingly resilient. Despite its fragility and low esteem, much survived. Remnants and memories of past glories inspired many of today's neon artists and fertilized fresh growth. Many are old enough to remember the excitement of a glittery downtown, of cruising the strip on Saturday night, of driving cross-country and reaching the oasis of a neon-lit small town or motel.

There is more to its appeal than simple nostalgia. Neon has the quality that distinguishes vintage animated films from the computer-generated cartoons of Saturday-morning television: it is hand drawn, not stamped out. A suggestive outline by day; at night it can appear as a line of liquid fire, a sensuous trickle of color, a pyrotechnic display. It can either carry the entire story or play a supporting role. This book celebrates the magic and diversity of neon, and some of the many craftsmen, designers, and artists who have used it inventively.

History and Technique

Neon lighting was introduced by Georges Claude in Paris in 1910, following decades of experiments to create a practical alternative to incandescent lighting. Claude's breakthrough was the development of a noncorroding, long-lasting electrode. This he patented, and for twenty years the Claude Neon Company enjoyed a near monopoly, selling franchises worldwide.

At the outbreak of World War Two, there were 2,000 neon sign companies in the United States employing 5,000 glass benders. It is estimated that there are only 300 benders who are still active, many of them nearing retirement. Courses in neon fabrication are being offered but, according to veteran craftsmen, it takes years of practice to master glass bending.

The fabrication of neon has changed little over the past seventy years. Everything is still done by hand. Glass tubes are heated over a flame, and bent to correspond to the design which has been drawn on an asbestos sheet. Electrodes are fused to either end of the tube, and the air is partly evacuated through a tiny vent. The tube is cleansed by bombarding it with up to 30,000 volts ("which is what they use for executions," remarks one bender). The loosened impurities and remaining air are removed by vacuum pump. An inert gas—usually neon, or argon mixed with a little mercury—is introduced, and the tube is sealed. A transformer feeds about 15,000 volts to the electrodes, and this causes the gas to ionize and hence to glow brightly with a steady light. A well-made tube will last thirty years or more, functioning far longer and at much lower cost than incandescent lighting.

In recent years, the technology has advanced, largely through the intervention of artists with a scientific bent. Microprocessors and solid-state circuitry have displaced mechanical animation; smaller, lighter transformers have been developed; high-frequency radio waves have been used to ionize the gas, freeing the tubes from their dependence on wires and electrodes.

Each gas has a distinctive color. Neon gives a fiery orange-red; argon enhanced with vaporized mercury, a brilliant blue. Argon by itself is a soft lavender. Other inert gases—krypton, xenon and helium—are expensive and are rarely used. In the heyday of neon, tubing in forty different colors was manufactured; many of these, including ruby red, midnight blue, uranium green and noviol gold, are no longer available. Artists hoard small quantities of these classic colors, but a majority of users make do with clear tubing that has been coated on the inside with phosphors that interact with the gas.

Over 150 colors can be achieved by combining different gases and phosphors. Artists have used tubing imported from Europe: the colors are distinctive, but the glass is more brittle than the American variety. Others have painted clear tubing to achieve as wide a range of color as any artist; more durable enamels are being developed for outdoor use.

Vintage commercial signs in the 1976 Smithsonian exhibition, A Nation of Nations, *Washington, DC.* Photo by © Charles H. Phillips

Signs

2   Artist Larry Rivers said it well: "Neon has gaiety, joy, pageantry. Circus qualities. The canvas is the night. Neon is the simplest and strongest form of illustration." And, he might have added, an unmatched medium for advertising.

It began with lettering. A Parisian barber is supposed to have put up the first neon nameplate, in 1912. By 1914, there were 160 neon signs in Paris; later, the Eiffel Tower served Citroen as the world's tallest billboard. Earl C. Anthony purchased two neon signs in Paris in 1923, and installed them over his Packard showroom in Los Angeles. They were the first to be seen in America and, for a time, they stopped traffic. At this stage, novelty was a sufficient draw; the designs were unremarkable. It was in the following decade that neon began to realize its full potential. It was used for decoration and to convey messages—from airplane wings, the Goodyear blimp, a neon-outlined repair truck, and as Stepin Fetchit's signature on his pink Rolls Royce.

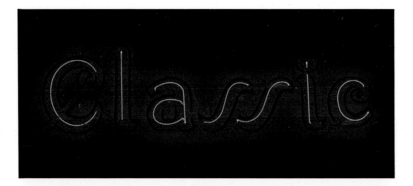

Classic Cleaners (1937), Salt Lake City.

Roxy Theater (ca. 1936), Glendale, California.

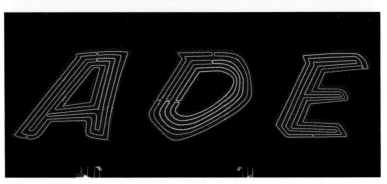

Ade Plumbers (1950s), Los Angeles.

4

Crenshaw Ford (1945), Los Angeles.

Vintage lettering offers an anthology of period style: streamline and geometrical deco, the juicy swirls of the 'forties, spiky mannerisms that echo the chrome flashes and automobile tail fins of the 'fifties. Images are equally revealing of period: ballroom dancers locked in perpetual embrace, a tubular bellhop, a Lionel model train, a muffler shop rocket, and a Flying Saucer cafe. These custom designs were accompanied by variations on the stock repertoire of shoes, fish, keys, and cocktail glasses; Mexicans dozing beside cacti and sombreros propped on guitars. An extinct species, now eagerly collected, was the neon clock—many of which were made by one company, in Lima, Ohio.

6 In the 1946 feature, *The Best Years of Our Lives,* a returning solider exclaims: "Look, he's got a new neon sign!", and neon symbolized his—and the audience's—release from wartime austerity. Art critic William Wilson described neon as: "the magic wand that gave downtown its boogie-woogie spirit, etching the edges of buildings, embroidering tapestries of light."

Times Square was the apotheosis of that spirit. Every town had its animated signs: puffing pipes and dripping faucets, firebreathing dragons and girls diving into motel pools. At their best, they transcended the monotony of on/off to achieve a compelling rhythm. But they were small scale and scattered. Times Square was outdoor theater on a scale that Max Reinhardt might have envied, its facades the stage for the animated spectaculars of Artkraft-Strauss.

Holly's Restaurant (1953), Los Angeles.

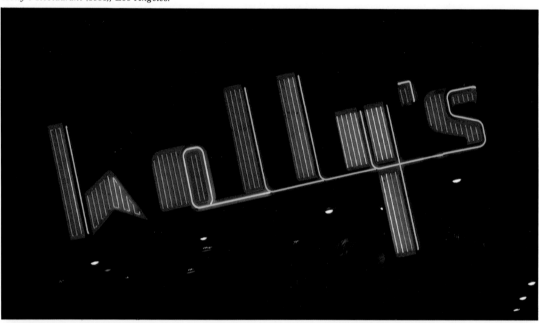

Stardust Hotel (1957) designed by Young Electric Sign Co. [Yesco], Las Vegas

Sundance Casino (1977, design by Yesco),
Las Vegas.

8   The Artkraft-Strauss Company achieved its dominance through the combination of a talented designer, Douglas Leigh, and the technical wizardry of Jacob Starr. Times Square had been ablaze with incandescent lights since the 1910s—the culmination of the Great White Way. Leigh and Starr gave it the neon signs that are still fondly remembered, beginning in the mid-'thirties and continuing through the 'fifties. They included the Wrigley boy, floating on a pack of spearmint, surrounded by fish blowing bubbles, and Budweiser's eagle flapping its wings above a team of animated Clydesdales. An eight-storey Little Lulu drew a Kleenex from its box; Johnny Walker strode untiringly; the aroma of coffee wafted down from a neon cup. When war broke out, the signs were extinguished; their light was so intense that they silhouetted ships miles out to sea, making them an easy target for German submarines.

Frank the Trainman (1946), San Diego

New California Motel (1930s), San Diego

Panaieff Ballet Center (1940), Hollywood. The founder—Michael Panaieff of the Ballet Russes de Monte Carlo—was the model.

A & M Muffler Shop (1957), San Diego

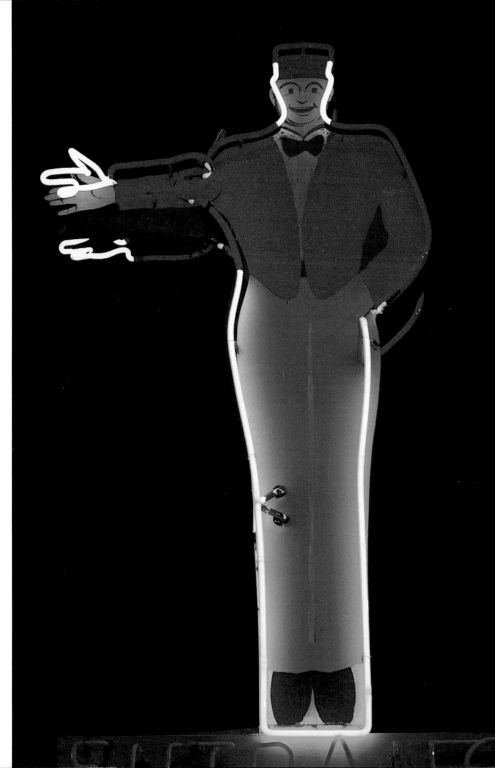

Larry's Hot Dogs (ca. 1950), Burbank, California.

Nathan's Famous (1933), Coney Island, Brooklyn, New York.

Howard Johnson's "Simple Simon" (1949), New York.

10

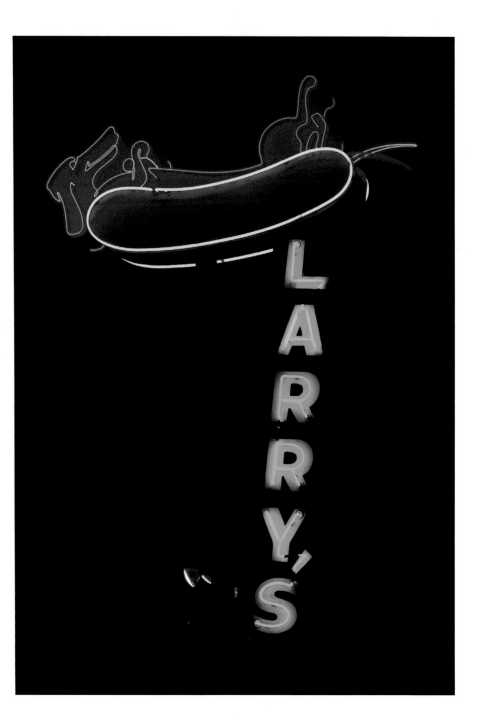

Pig Sandwich (1930), Houston.

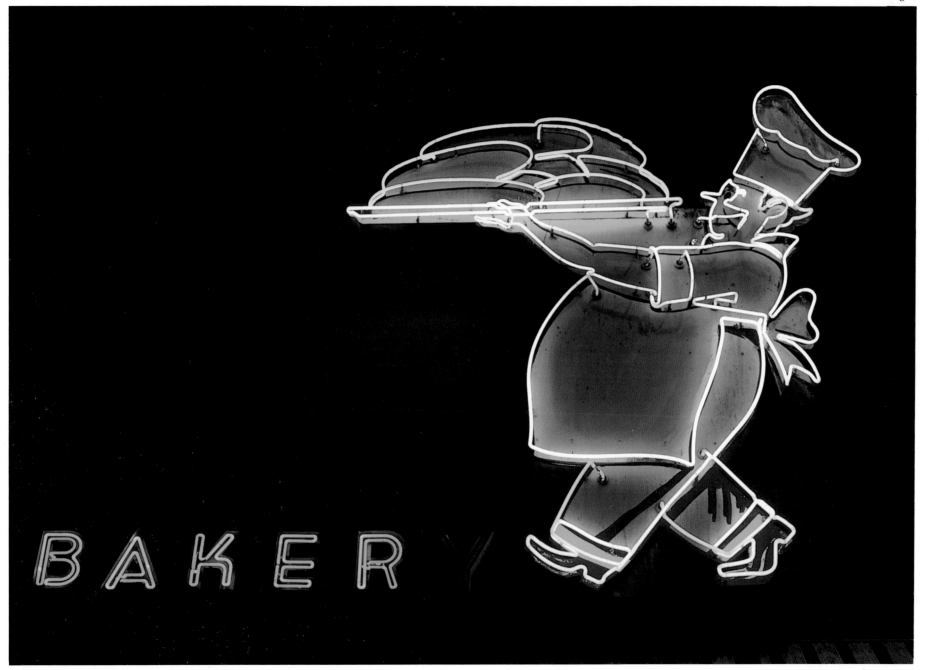

Canter's Bakery (1951), Los Angeles.

12

*Wagon Wheel Restaurant and Motel
(1930s), Oxnard, California.*

Dublin House Bar (1933), New York.

Earl Scheib Auto Painting (1950s), Beverly Hills, California.

14

Felix Chevrolet (1957), Los Angeles. The updated television image of the popular movie cartoon character of the 'twenties.

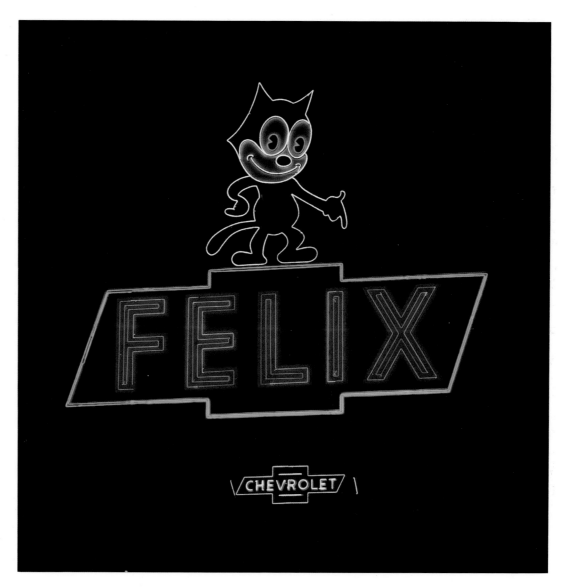

Firebreathing Trio

Golden Dragon Restaurant (1950s),
Chinatown, New York.

Star Noodle Restaurant (ca. 1950), Ogden,
Utah.

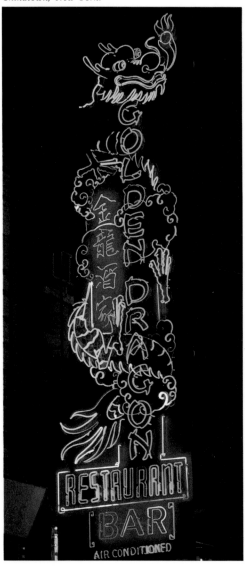

Detail of Chinese Theater marquee (1958),
Hollywood.

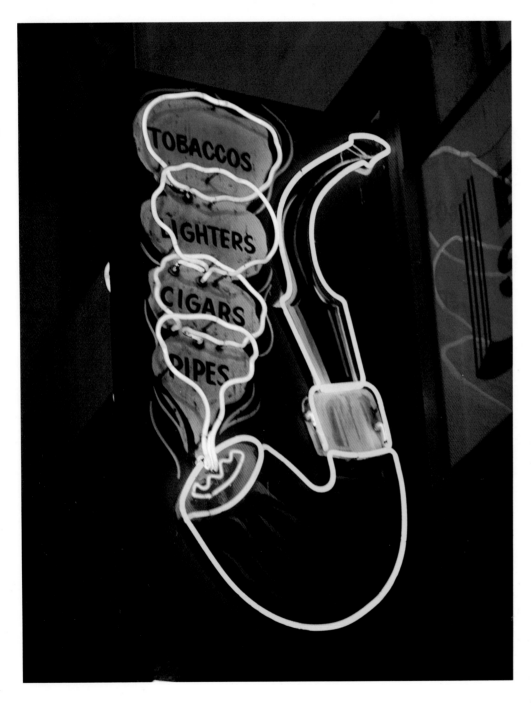

Animated Classics

John's Pipe Store (ca. 1940), Hollywood

Clayton Plumbers (1947), West Los Angeles.

Steele's Motel (ca. 1950), Van Nuys, California.

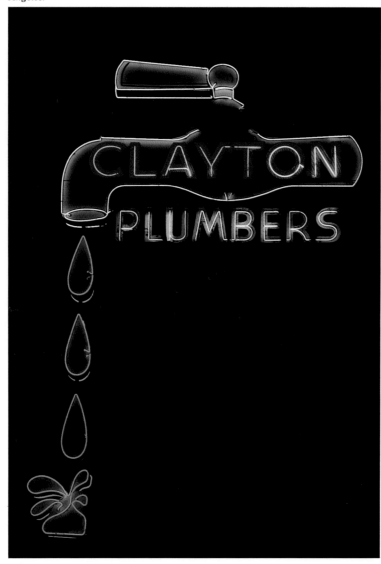

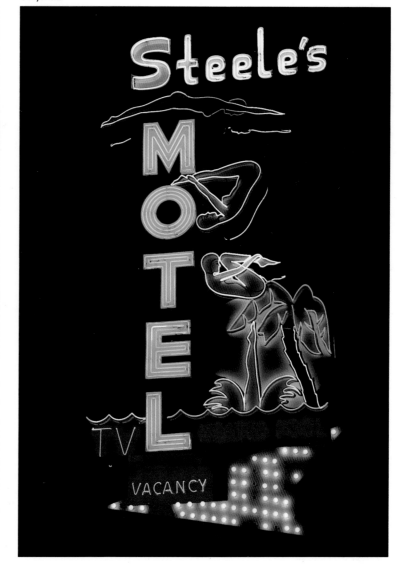

5th Street Liquor (ca. 1950), Las Vegas.

Pied Piper Pest Control (1950s), San Diego.

Animation by Day

*Sea and Jungle Imports (1952), Glendale,
California.*

22

Pioneer Club cowboy (1951, design by Yesco).

Times Square today (like Hong Kong, and Tokyo's Ginza) is notable more for the quantity that the quality of its neon. Its former inventiveness has been transposed to Las Vegas. There, as Tom Wolfe noted, the signs upstage the buildings. "They revolve, they oscillate, they soar—in shapes before which the existing vocabulary of art history is helpless." Neon is only one of the stars in this electrographic extravaganza, but it has some great roles: The giant cowboy and cowgirl that guard Fremont Street; the orgastic surges of the Dunes' arch and palm trees; the palpitating feathers of the Flamingo's huge pink bird.

At the heart of the Strip, neon has been overwhelmed by plastics. The heraldic symbols of the major hotels rest uncomfortably atop back-lit panels announcing the week's entertainment and bargain breakfasts. Further on, in the cheaper section, is an enchanted grove of wedding chapels and motels, each seeking to differentiate itself with a potent neon image. The richest concentration of neon is downtown, on Fremont Street.

In 1982, a storm blacked out the city. Only the Strip, linked to emergency generators, continued to blaze. From the approaching car or plane, it must have seemed more than ever a mirage in the desert, as improbable (in Reyner Banham's felicitous phrase) as "a human base camp on a hostile planet."

The quest for bigger and brighter signs began with the emergence of Las Vegas as a gambler's paradise in the mid-forties. Today, there are ten major sign companies; then there was one— Young Electric, a Mormon family firm, based in Salt Lake City. There is a pleasing irony in the fact that Mormons helped found Las Vegas on their westward trek to the promised land, then returned nearly a century later to give it a new identity. Thomas Young, Sr. sketched the first big animated sign on Fremont Street (for the Boulder Club, later replaced by The Mint) in 1946; then set up shop to service its rivals.

The Strip was launched in the same year, when gangster Bugsy Siegel established the Flamingo. Tom Wolfe, the Berenson of kitsch, described its first incarnation: "Two cylinders rose at either end. . . covered from top to bottom with neon rings in the shape of bubbles that fizzed all eight stories up into the desert sky like an illuminated whisky-soda tumbler filled to the brim with pink champagne."

By day, the Strip seems oppressive. It is cluttered and pretentious; its former roadhouses submerged in a tide of mirror glass and *portes cocheres* as large as football fields. Twilight transforms this seedy Sodom into a magic garden of exotic blooms, which tint the air, dematerialize the architecture, and turn its slick surfaces into a reflective crazy quilt.

24

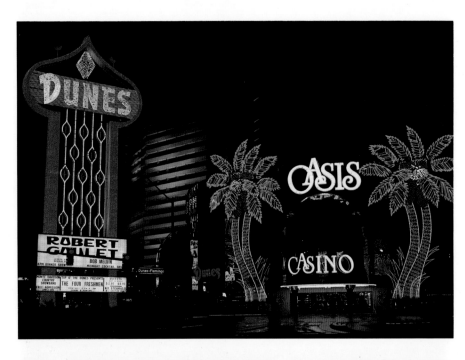

Dunes Hotel (1963, design by Federal Sign & Signal) and Oasis Casino (1982, design by Ad-Art).

Flamingo facade (1978, design by Heath & Co.).

Signs on the Strip

Las Vegas has done more than pro-voke moral outrage and pop prose. It is an inspiration to those who would restore color and fantasy to the darkened streets of other American cities. Spurred by Venturi and Scott Brown's *Learning from Las Vegas*, archi-tects and designers are acquiring a new respect for the vernacular, and are turn-ing away from schematic utopias to reinterpret the past. There is a popular reaction against stuffy good taste and sterile plazas, away from "beautifica-tion" and master plans, towards the cheerful vitality of restored and recycled old buildings.

Flamingo Hilton (1975, design by Ad-Art).

China Club Restaurant-Lounge (1980,
design by April Greiman).

Trendy Revivalism

Neon is a key component in this new aesthetic, a beacon to the young and the sophisticated. Nowhere is this trendy revivalism, with its knowing references to 'thirties deco and 'fifties funk, so evident as in Los Angeles. Along Melrose Avenue and neighboring streets, new wave boutiques boast signs that are as offbeat as their names. Cadillac Ranch, Vinyl Fetish, the China Club, Strip Thrills and The Ghost of Romaine Brooks achieve their effects through mannered typography and novel color combinations. Other signs, including High Tech and Flip, update traditional forms of animation. Neon is looped like streamers around the proscenium of Melon's, and serves as an art nouveau border for the antiques of De Luxe. In New York, neon's use as signage seems less developed, but it has been employed inventively in window displays—most notably in a 1978 series at Tiffany's.

Cadillac Ranch vintage clothing (1979, design by Charles di Bona).

Vinyl Fetish records (1980, design by Paul Greenstein).

Let it Rock 'fifties clothes (1981, design by Paul Greenstein).

Strip Thrills clothing (1973).

Flipper's Roller Boogie Palace (1979).

*The Ghost of Romaine Brooks fine prints
(1982, design by Lili Lakich), Los Angeles.*

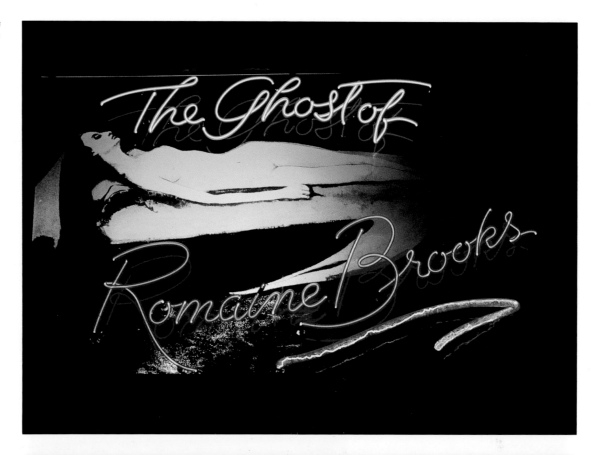

Strawberries Records (1979), Boston.

30   Neon's linearity makes it a natural ally of graphics—as art work for record albums, billboards and posters and, as here, for book covers. The entire campaign for the movie *Victor Victoria* was keyed to neon. The original intention was to reproduce actual neon; for lack of funds the effect was simulated with paint—on the poster, trailer and main titles—and it achieved a convincing illusion of the real thing. Neon was employed for the original logos of *A Chorus Line* and *Sophisticated Ladies*. For the movie version of *Zoot Suit*, the process was reversed. A big neon sign portrayed a jitterbugging couple over the theater marquee, drawing on the graphic art that had achieved recognition during the play's year-long run.

Animated riverboat (1983, design by Brad Jirka), is the 24-foot-long centerpiece of the Riverplace Development, Minneapolis.
Photo by © Marc Norberg

*Flip vintage clothing (1981, design by
Peter Watson), West Hollywood.*

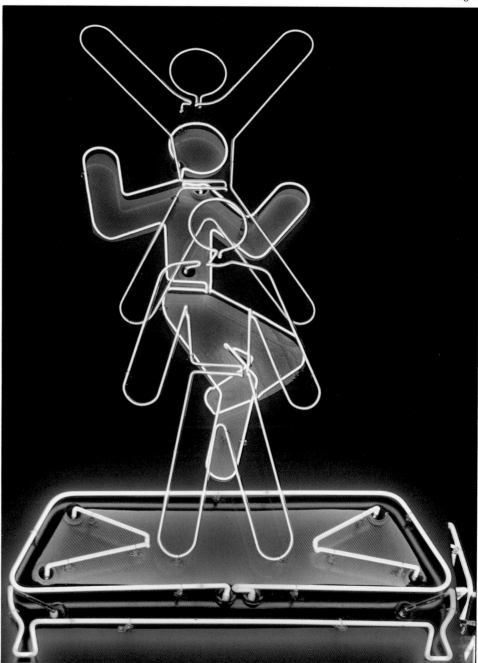

*High Tech gymnastic equipment (1981,
design by Lili Lakich), West Hollywood.*

De Luxe antiques (1979, design by Charles di Bona)

Melon's fashions (1982, designed by Kenneth Vorzimer and Richard Lehman, Century Group)

Miniature neon display in the windows of Tiffany's, New York (1978, design by John Tanaka). Courtesy Tiffany's

Custom Neon, Los Angeles, is one of many such workshop/stores across the country.

Decor

34   Neon has played featured roles in Hollywood for the past fifty years. Busby Berkeley, the drill instructor turned dance director, introduced it into the production numbers of such 'thirties musicals as *Gold Diggers of 1933* and *Dames*. His chorines endured the occasional shock to play neon-edged violins and pianos, and bathe in neon-backed tubs. Studio-bound gangster movies evoked city streets by the flash of a neon sign. A recent feature, *Fame*, used the same device, blocking the view from a student's room with a section of the Times Square Coca Cola sign.

Production number from Dames, *a 1934 Warner Brothers musical.* Courtesy of Richard Jenkins

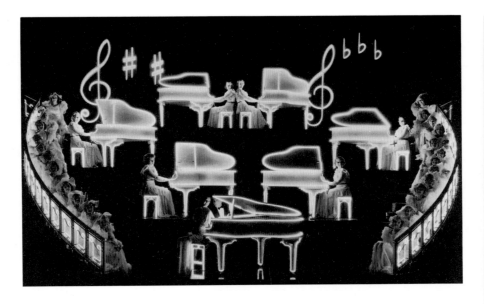

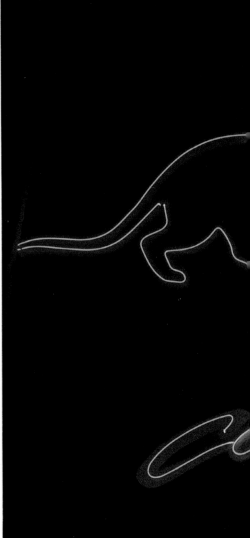

Cat People *(1982, design by Rod Dyer; Universal Pictures release)*

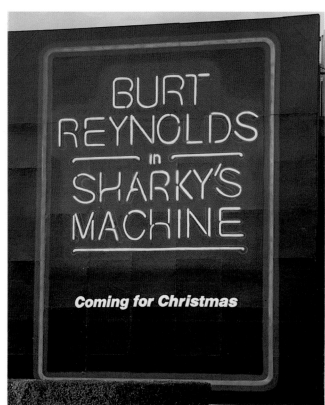

Sharky's Machine *(1981, design by Larry Noble and Eddie Vartanian, Orion/Warner Brothers release)*

36   In other recent productions, neon has been used to establish period. Steven Spielberg's *1941* deployed miniatures of vintage signs on a model of Hollywood Boulevard; a replica of the classic sign for Rick's Cafe was featured in the television version of *Casablanca*. Ridley Scott's *Blade Runner* transposed a 'forties private eye drama to a nightmarish city of the future. Neon was used to light and ornament narrow studio streets, creating a carapace of flashing lights that pressed in aggressively from every side. Scott and production designer Lawrence Paull sought inspiration in the bazaars of Tokyo and Hong Kong, and the sex shops of Times Square, to achieve a sense of claustrophobia and overload.

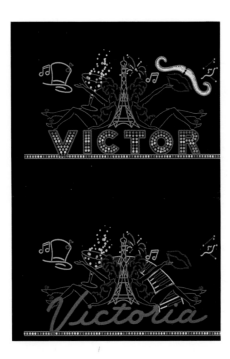

Trailer art for the movie Victor Victoria *(1982, design by Lili Lakich; campaign by Intralink; MGM release).* Courtesy Intralink.

"You must remember this..." The classic Rick's Cafe sign, reincarnated for the David L. Wolper television version of Casablanca *(1982, production designer Preston Ames)*

Blade Runner: *neon-bejewelled man-nequin.* Courtesy The Ladd Company

The Los Angeles street at the Burbank Studios, dressed for the production of Blade Runner *(1981, production designer Lawrence Paull; Ladd Company production).* Courtesy The Ladd Company

38

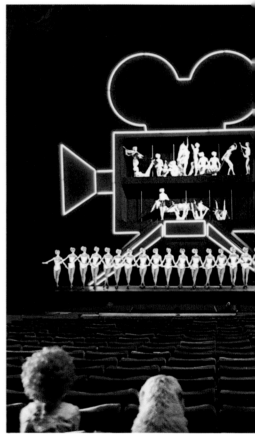

Francis Coppola's *One from the Heart* superimposed one fantasy upon another, by recreating Las Vegas on the stages of Zoetrope Studios in Hollywood. Production designer Dean Tavoularis used ten miles of neon in a series of sets that were at times astonishingly close to the real thing, at others an entrancing stylization. Neon expressed the brittle gaiety and surface masquerade of people and place. It beckoned from the end of the block like the Land of Oz. It made you believe that an ocean liner was moored in the desert; that a girl could emerge from a flashing sign, walk a high wire over a surreal junkyard, and frolic in a luminous cocktail glass.

Neon is indispensable for special effects. It runs cool and its intensity can be varied: crucial concerns when shooting miniatures, one frame at a time, with exposures of several seconds each. Neon artist Larry Albright has made a second career of simulating intergalactic weaponry and UFOs in such movies as *Close Encounters of the Third Kind*, *Star Trek* and *Battlestar Galactica*, in addition to creating the miniature signs for *1941* and for the title sequence of *One from the Heart*.

Neon set on the stage of Radio City Music Hall, from the movie Annie *(1982, production designer Dale Hennesy; Rastar production, Columbia release).* Courtesy Columbia Pictures

Composite art work created to publicize One from the Heart *(1982, production designer Dean Tavoularis; Zoetrope Studios production).* Courtesy Francis Coppola

Television Design

Television commercial for Frito Lay (1983, design by Jeffrey Howard)

Television art directors use neon to achieve dramatic illusions, quickly and at low cost. Maris Ozolins designed a commercial for Burlington Industries in which a bed appeared to float on a neon cloud, and an endless neon road for a Toyota spot. For a Frito Lay commercial, Jeffrey Howard designed a backdrop of floating bags, their painted images highlighted with colored tubing. The razzle-dazzle of neon sustains the excitement on game shows and dance contests.

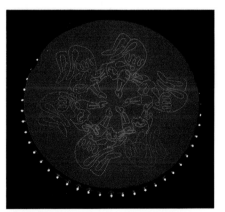

Whirling neon symbol for television game show, The Joker's Wild *(1981, design by John Mula)*

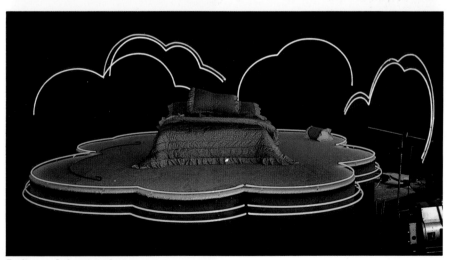

Burlington Industries television commercial (1982, design by Maris Ozolins)

Stage Sets by Tony Walton

The Cotton Club set (1981).
Courtesy *Sophisticated Ladies*

40

Few designers have used neon, on screen and stage, as effectively as Tony Walton. He created an Oz-like New York for Sidney Lumet's film of *The Wiz*, using hot reds and purples for the "hookers' heaven" scene, in which the Poppy Love Perfume Company lures its victims through luscious lips and down a smoke-filled pink neon throat. Walton borrowed the idea of the lips puffing smoke from the old Camels sign on Times Square.

In his sets for *Chicago* and *Sophisticated Ladies*, Walton used neon to evoke atmosphere. For *Chicago*, producer Bob Fosse wanted a tough yet stylish look. Black vinyl and chrome mesh provided a hard, glittery surface, whose apparent solidity dissolved when the neon, concealed within, was switched on. Neon images—the main title, a sunburst marquee, a stylized dance band—heralded different scenes. A similar idea was employed in *Sophisticated Ladies*, but there the lighting was attached to scrims, not contained within a standing set. Each component was lowered in turn or in combination: a deco border, a train, a plane, a jungle with winking eyes, the fire escapes and club signs of Harlem—as leitmotifs for specific numbers and as a complement to the exuberant dancing and the music of Duke Ellington's band.

Chicago (1975): Chita Rivera and Gwen Verdon in "Vaudeville Finale."
Courtesy Tony Walton

Movie Theater Marquees

42   The concept of the frame as symbol was first exploited in the theater marquee, and developed in the movie palaces. As architect S. Charles Lee declared: "the show begins on the sidewalk." The avant-garde Titania Palast in Berlin had a neon-lit tower and marquee in the late 'twenties; by the mid 'thirties, neon had begun to replace the original incandescent-lit marquees, and moveable neon letters were sometimes used to announce the current attractions. Geometrical neon marquees were the major decorative feature of the plainer, Depression-era theaters.

The frisky dragons of the Chinese Theater in Hollywood; the Laurelhurst in Portland, Oregon; Dallas' Inwood and Esquire, and Seattle's Collisseum are among the notable survivors. The Joyce Theater in New York (recently converted from movies to dance) uses neon to accent and back-light a neo-deco marquee and glass brick facade. Drive-in screens did double duty as giant signs. The Campus in San Diego boasted a fifty-foot-high neon tableau of a majorette twirling her baton against a backdrop of the neighboring university. It is now in storage, awaiting a new owner.

Marquee for the Chinese Theater, Hollywood. One of two animated dragons added to the original facade in 1958

Nuart, West Los Angeles. Animated geometry on a plain thirties box

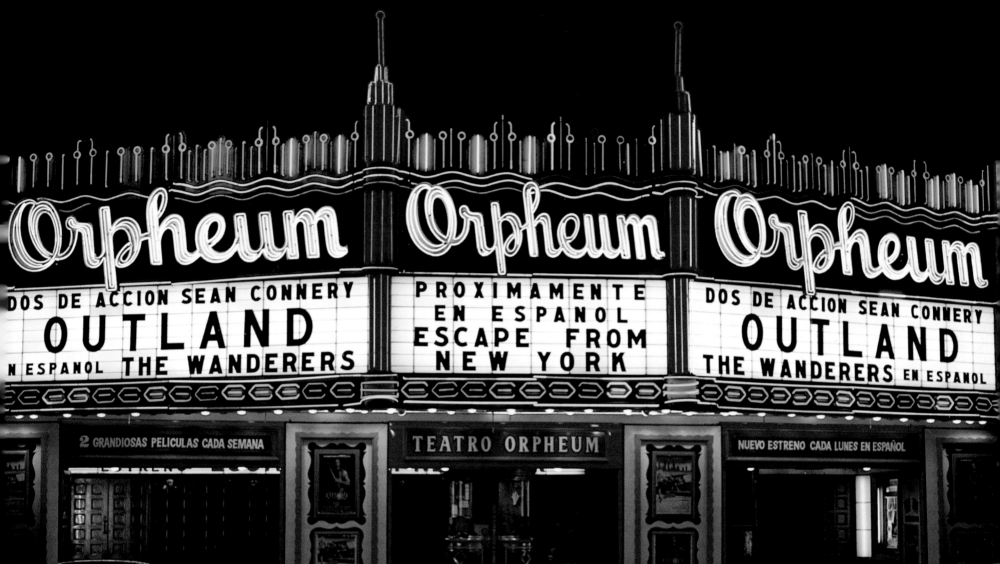

Esquire (1940s), Dallas. Photo © David Naylor

Colisseum (1950), Seattle. The tower, with its tableau of a musical production, used to revolve. Photo © Alan Berner

44

Joyce Theater (1982), New York. A dance space, remodelled from the old Elgin Theater by Hardy Holzman Pfeiffer.

Campus Drive-In (1946), San Diego. A spectacular piece, now in storage, whose majorette twirled her baton against a backdrop of San Diego State University

Chrysler Building spire, New York. Veteran designer Douglas Leigh installed fluorescent tubes in place of the neon originally planned, as part of the 1982 restoration

Zig-Zag Revisited

In 1937, the Eiffel Tower was embroidered with 32,000 feet of pink, blue and green neon, to celebrate an international exposition. Since then, neon has outlined government buildings in pre-revolutionary Teheran, royal palaces in Saudi Arabia, diners, motels and Chinatown pagodas—even a tombstone for someone's dog. Fluorescent tubes stand in for neon on the spire of New York's Chrysler Building, and accent the zig-zag ornamentation of a theater in Beverly Hills.

Beverly Theater, Beverly Hills. White neon put up in 1982 replaces the original tubing

*Golden Pagoda Restaurant (1938), Chinatown,
Los Angeles*

*Aerospace Historical Center, Balboa Park, San
Diego. Formerly the Ford Pavilion, it was
designed by Walter Dorwin Teague for the
1935 California Pacific International
Exposition*

50

52

Tokyo's Ginza is wall-to-wall neon, a counterpart of downtown Las Vegas, where the signs create an architecture of light, and the Golden Nugget Casino is concealed behind a baroque facade of animated tubing. An office tower on John Street in lower Manhattan is entered through a tunnel of blue neon, and a sensuous palette of color highlights Charles Moore's Piazza d'Italia in New Orleans. Another architect, Herbert Newman, proposed an animated neon horse race to run around the drum-like Teletrack Theater, next to Interstate 95 in New Haven. That proved too costly, but the neon band that was substituted serves as a landmark for incoming planes, and the original concept has been adapted for use as a wall graphic inside.

Architecture of light: Fremont Street in downtown Las Vegas

Caesar's Palace, Las Vegas. Neon-lit porte cochere *was added in 1978. Design by Yesco*

St. Joseph's Fountain, Piazza d'Italia (1978, architect Charles Moore with Urban Innovations Group, Ronald Filson; and with Allen Eskew and Malcolm Heard of Perez Associates), New Orleans.
Photo © Norman McGrath

Interior Lighting

54

Neon was a fashionable form of interior lighting in the 'thirties. S. Charles Lee used it for cove lighting (painting the tubes with a red stripe to achieve a flattering quality of light) and ran a sunken strip of neon down the aisles of the 1931 Los Angeles Theater to guide patrons in the dark. During the Depression, when work was short, he amused himself by creating neon-stemmed cocktail glasses that lit up when placed on the bar. The lobby of Hollywood's Earl Carroll Theater (1938) was lit by neon encased in glass rods that surrounded the columns and the base of the bar. A whiplash of tubing ran through the hands of a silvered nude and up to the ceiling. Architect John Seibel is currently restoring the glamor that was epitomised by Carroll's original neon sign, which read: "Through these portals pass the most beautiful girls in the world."

Neon graphic in Teletrack Theater (1980, Herbert Newman Associates), New Haven, Connecticut. Photo © Norman McGrath

Lobby of the Earl Carroll theater, Hollywood (1938). Courtesy David Gebhart

*Backstreet Restaurant (1980, architect Mark
Simon of Moore Grover Harper),
New Haven, Connecticut.*
Photo © Norman McGrath

*Mural in The Warehouse (1982, design by
Petrie Fishman and Alison Witt), Chicago.*
Courtesy Lightwriters Neon

56

Fat City interior (1982, design by Anthony Machado)

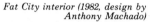

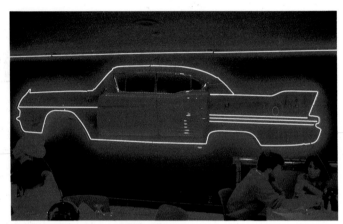

Fat City. Doors from a 1958 Cadillac are outlined in neon as one of several pop sculptures (Design by Anthony Machado)

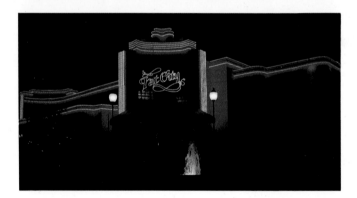

Fat City Restaurant (1981, design by Robert Miller, Harbor Sign and Lighting), San Diego

Streamline moderne—with its associations of luxury liners and sophisticated night clubs—inspires contemporary designers. New York's Century Cafe features a recycled movie marquee over the bar; down in Soho, neon lighting enhances the all-pink decor of Wings restaurant. Another fashionable eating place, the Backstreet in New Haven, has a city facade of streetlamps and skyscrapers that is reflected in mirrors on the back wall, and echoed by swirls of neon on the ceiling. In Chicago, Ellen Sandor has created a series of luminous erotic tableaux for Nick's restaurant.

San Diego's Fat City restaurant goes the limit. The original streamline exterior was painted pink, and outlined with red and blue tubes. Designer Anthony Machado enlivened the narrow, low-ceilinged interior with a marvellously eclectic mixture of neon-edged columns and portholes, backed with blue fabric to create a rosy hue, and glass room dividers filled with multicolored balls that reflect the light. Neon runs around the room and is used to accent pop sculptures: a Winged Victory, a sailfish, and the doors of a Pepto-Bismol pink 1958 Cadillac.

58

Emerald City Disco (1979), Cherry Hill, New Jersey. Twenty sequential circuits of multicolored neon are contained within the glass brick wall. Lighting by Design Circuit International. Photo © Doug Wright/John Bellissimo

Even this audacious decor seems gently romantic when set beside the latest discotheques. Here, the goal of the lighting is to create a visual interpretation of the music, to accent the rhythm, and to enhance the mood of the dancers. The audience is young, fickle and demanding; the audio-visual rhythms must stir the blood and move the feet.

No-one understands this better than Robert Lobi, a 'sixties musician turned lighting designer, who established Design Circuit International in New York, ten years ago. The firm has designed spectacular interiors world-wide; its most ambitious was the now-defunct Emerald City Disco in Cherry Hill, New Jersey. Up to 2000 dancers could be acommodated on the huge black parquet floor. The focal point was a tower and two-tier wall of glass brick, back-lit with 20 channels of sequential neon. A steel and acrylic "emerald" atop the tower rotated, flashing a beam of light over the dancers. Two channels of light in glass-covered trenches raced across the floor.

Overhead were neon-rimmed chandeliers and a whirligig of red and blue neon rockets. These and many more installations were activated by a "light musician" playing a bioelectric keyboard that resembled a xylophone. As Lobi described it: "we created a stage on which everyone could be a star."

Design Circuit also did the lighting for two notable clubs in New York: the Copacabana, with its starburst ceiling and neon-fronded plaster palm trees, and the Starship Discovery, in which bolts of lightning flashed across the ceiling and down a central column.

Another talented design group, Neon New York, which lit the interior of Wings, contributed a dramatic light sculpture to the entrance hall of Studio 54, suspending argon tubes from a crystal chandelier and running them out to wall mirrors. For the Starbucks Disco, they established a Western theme, outlining mesas around the walls, and lighting the elevator with a plexiglass-enclosed neon peyote flower.

Copacabana *(1980), New York. Animated neon fronds were added to the existing plaster palm trees by Design Circuit International.* Photo © Doug Wright/John Bellissimo

Xanadunes game room in the Dunes's Oasis Casino (1982, design by Yesco), Las Vegas

Starship Discovery (1978), New York. Lightning bolts flash over the dance floor and down the central column. Created by Design Circuit International. Photo © Doug Wright/John Bellissimo

Art

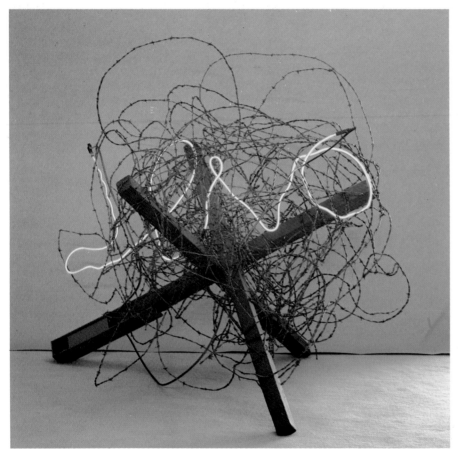

James Rosenquist: Tumbleweed *(1964-66, collection of Mr. and Mrs. Bagley Wright, Seattle).* Photo © Paul M. Macapia

Neon had been around for fifty years before artists made much use of it. As early as the twenties, Dadaists employed mundane materials for their shock value, Constructivists sought to integrate art with the machine, the Bauhaus explored what Gyorgy Kepes termed "the fluid power of light in action." Laszlo Moholy-Nagy created a motorized metal and glass sculpture, *Light-Space Modulator* (1922-30). Oskar Schlemmer attempted, in his theater workshop at the Bauhaus, to dematerialize space with changing colors and lights. Thomas Wilfred, a Danish artist who settled in New York, worked with projected light from the thirties on. thirties on.

Neon would have been an ideal medium for these and other innovative artists. But, aside from the large-scale ambient neons that Lucio Fontana created around 1950, it was not until the sixties that artists began to exploit neon's luminous, kinetic, and defiantly antitraditional properties. By then, commercial neon was in sharp decline, its prestige at a low ebb. Pop art rescued it from the junk pile, just as it offered a fresh perspective on much else that was commonly despised. Artists such as George Segal, Jasper Johns, Robert Rauschenberg and James Rosenquist used neon—but only as a minor element in their work, or for an isolated piece, such as Rosenquist's *Tumbleweed* (1964-66) and Rauschenberg's neon drawing *Green Shirt* (1965-67), which was displayed outdoors at the Pasadena Museum of Art.

It was an immigrant Greek artist, *Chryssa*, who first exploited neon as an expressive medium. Soon after settling in New York in 1954, Chryssa declared: "America is very stimulating, intoxicating for me. . . the vulgarity of America as seen in the lights of Times Square is poetic, very poetic. A foreigner can describe this. Americans feel it." Beginning in 1962, Chryssa refined and redefined this poetic vulgarity in a series of "neon boxes": an alignment of repetitive shapes, based on a letter of the alphabet, set on a pedestal-transformer within a tinted plexiglass box. Like the signs that inspired them, they flashed on and off—but the calligraphy was stylized, the effect elegant and mysterious.

The artist described these boxes—and pieces that combined neon with metal channel letters—as studies for major work: *The Gates of Times Square* (1964-66), a ten-foot cube of steel, plexiglass, lights, and neon that is now displayed at the Albright-Knox Art Gallery in Buffalo, New York. Critic Robert Hughes described her work of this period as: "a chimerical amalgam of cultures, as though we were looking back on Times Square from a vantage point as remote in time from it as ours is from ancient Greece. The signs have ceased to signify. They are. . . archaic fragments."

Chryssa subsequently developed other themes in neon: *Clytemnestra* (based on her impression of Irene Papas's stage gestures), *Flight of Birds*, and *Automat* (derived from Horn and Hardart's sign). In the seventies, she incorporated neon into modeled or painted surfaces: as a series of fragmented lines emerging from a design drawn on asbestos; as the accent to a grid of plastic letters.

Chryssa's achievement was crucial to the development of neon art. It encompassed the major concerns of a formative decade: pop imagery, language, minimalism, the dematerialization of solid objects, the role of light and movement. It offered an inspiring model, and suggested the three directions in which neon art was to move: words and images, light and color, kinetic and performance art.

Chryssa: Times Square Sky *(1962, collection of Walker Art Center, Minneapolis; gift of the T.B. Walker Foundation).* Photo © Walker Art Center

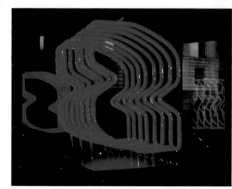

Chryssa: Clytemnestra *(1967), collection of the Corcoran Gallery of Art, Washington, DC.* Photo © Mark Gulezian, QuickSilver

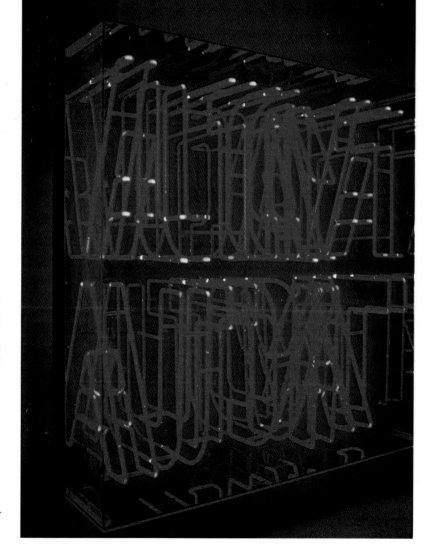

Chryssa: Automat *(1971, collection of Harry Abrams family).* Courtesy: Robert Abrams

62

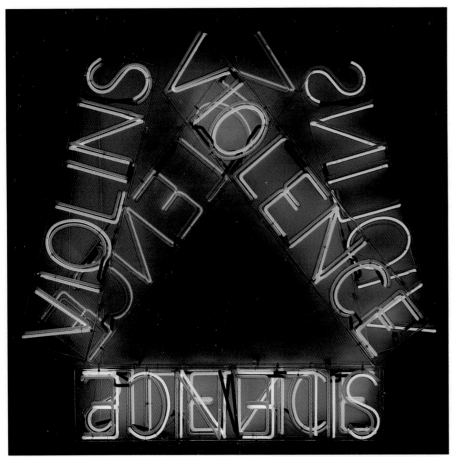

Bruce Nauman: Violins Violence Silence
*(1982, courtesy Leo Castelli Gallery, New
York, and Sperone Westwater Fischer Inc.,
New York).* Photo © Duane Suter,
Baltimore

Bruce Nauman could be described as the poet of signage. Beginning in 1966, and continuing to the present, he has used neon as a vehicle for words. Brenda Richardson, who curated a recent retrospective of Nauman's neons at the Baltimore Museum of Art, compares his neon signs with the word play of such artists as Warhol, Lichtenstein, and Ruscha, who also borrowed the forms of advertising to comment on society, and as materials with which to forge a work of art.

For Nauman, the commercial signs surrounding his San Francisco studio were a direct source of inspiration, and he displayed his first sign in the window where it could be casually observed by passers by. *Window or Wall Sign* (1967) reads: "The true artist helps the world by revealing mystic truths," in a red-outlined spiral of blue letters. As Nauman remarked: "It was just another neon on the street until someone paid attention. . . Then, when you read it, you would have to think about it."

Richardson describes one of his first uses of the medium, *Neon Templates of the Left Half of my Body, Taken at Ten Inch Intervals,* as "an abstract expressionist drawing in high relief." Another, *My Last Name Exaggerated 14 Times Vertically* (1967), transformed his signature into calligraphy as radically stylized as Chryssa's letters. His subse-

quent work ranged from wordplays to poems to a single word that was laden with resonance. *My Name as Though it Were Written on the Surface of the Moon* (1968) repeats each letter of "Bruce" as though they had been freed from the pull of gravity. Such word plays as RAW/WAR, NONE SING/NEON SIGN, RUN FROM FEAR/FUN FROM REAR exploit what Richardson calls "the duality of a seductive medium and a provocative thought."

Nauman's most recent neons, notably *American Violence* (1981-82) and *Violins Violence Silence* (1982) are more refined and complex than the early work, employing as many as twelve colors and a switching mechanism that flashes each word or phrase in turn. Nauman has a studio in New Mexico and travels extensively.

Lili Lakich uses neon as a magic crayon to create expressive portraits and tableaux—as well as commercial artwork and signs. Her love of neon was kindled by childhood memories of roadside signs (her family was always on the move) and strengthened by her exposure to the work of Chryssa, and the French pop artist Martial Raysse. She studied art at the Pratt Institute, learned the craft of neon by inquiring at sign companies, and began her career in New York in 1966. Two years later she moved to Los Angeles.

Lakich invests her work with emotion, wit and an outspokenly feminist attitude. Even her most stylized portraits are figurative, but they never lapse into the merely pictorial—a major pitfall for many self-styled neon artists. Whatever the starting point—a sailor's tattoo, a classic painting, traditional Mexican art—neon transforms the image or object with which it is juxtaposed. Her finest pieces have a poetic ambiguity. *Blessed Oblivion* (1975) portrays the death struggle of a python and panther within the framework of a Mexican tombstone. *Mona* (1981) is both a witty reworking of the *Mona Lisa,* and an appropriate image for the Museum of Neon Art that is temporarily housed in her studio. *Love in Vain* (1977) weaves a sinuous line around a silkscreened photograph, imbuing it with a sad yet dynamic quality. *Self Portrait with Sneer* (1977) fragments the lines to achieve an expressive effect.

She is equally adept at creating commercial signs (*High Tech, The Ghost of Romaine Brooks*) and simulated neon (a symbol for the new *Vanity Fair,* the trailer for *Victor Victoria*). And she creates neon pieces as the source for graphic imagery, as on the cover of this book and in her poster for an exhibition of women's art in Long Beach, California—which uses the head of the Statue of Liberty as a feminist symbol and as a playful domestic facade.

Lili Lakich: Blessed Oblivion *(1975, courtesy the artist)*

Lili Lakich: Love in Vain *(1977, courtesy the artist)*

64   *Stephen Antonakos* first used neon in assemblages of the late fifties, then switched to pure neon in 1962, the same year that Chryssa began to use it. These two Greek-born artists make an interesting contrast. She arrived in New York as a trained artist—and was swept away by American imagery; he came at age four and grew up in the city, yet his work has a purity of line and an intensity of light that speaks of the Mediterranean. "I love ancient Greek architecture, even the fragments," he declares, "but I like to see them outside, in the Greek light." And, to strengthen the connection: "I have always loved Matisse, especially the cut-outs... he took a simple idea and went far with it, making his forms and colors so alive."

Antonakos has explored what he describes as the "controlled paradise of neon" more profoundly than any other artist. Over the past twenty years he has, like Matisse, progressively simplified his forms with no sacrifice of feeling. He began with basic building blocks—lines, squares, and circles—in intense red and blue. These shapes were extended across walls, through corners, and into space. The geometry became more complex and then the process went into reverse. The shapes were fragmented and spaced more widely. The aggressive on/off programming and strong colors gave way to static, painterly compositions, utilizing softer colors. The viewer's eye was given the task of programming—as it adjusted to the natural vibration of the neon and the interplay between direct, diffused, and natural light.

In his most recent work, even the lines have a hand-drawn, three-dimensional quality. The compositions are defined by a textured panel or sheet

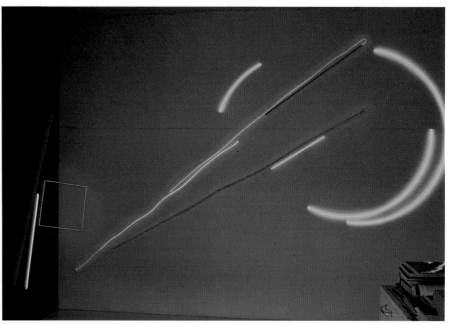

Stephen Antonakos: Untitled *(1982, courtesy the artist)*

of unstretched canvas; the surfaces are colored to complement the neon's hue and to create a haze of color around the viewer.

His studio pieces have grown more sensual and subtle, but Antonakos is creating dramatic, large-scale sculptures for streets and public buildings. As you emerge from the Lincoln Tunnel, New York City is heralded by fiery swirls of red neon on a blue wall, the centerpiece of Theater Row on West 42nd Street, just two blocks from Times Square. Other commissions include a geometrical frieze for the WPA Building in downtown Washington, D.C., and a four-part mural for Atlanta's new airport terminal. Most dramatic is the ceiling mural over the swimming pool of Hampshire College, in Amherst, Massachusetts. At night, the neon is reflected off the water and out through the glass walls, so that the entire building appears to be ablaze.

In other recent work, Antonakos has concealed neon beneath a white cube, so that it seems to float on an orange cloud of light, like an alien spaceship. It justifies his observation that, " . . . there seems to be a mystery about light, no matter how simple, direct, and clear one tries to make the idea. Through the years, you get closer and closer to this mystery, but it is always there."

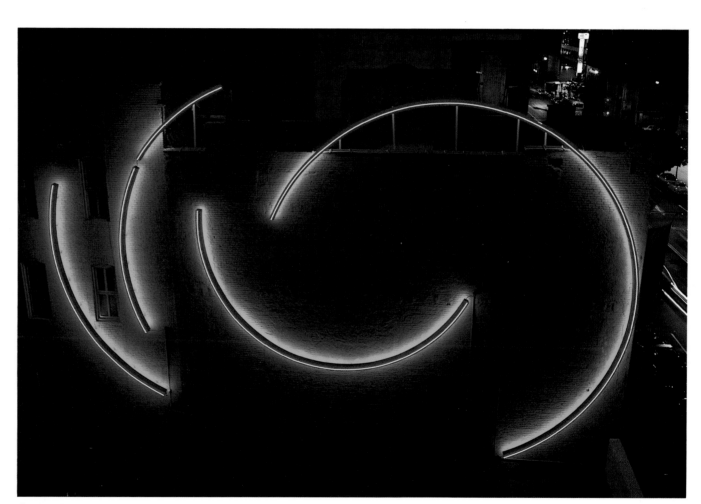

Stephen Antonakos's Neon for 42nd Street *(1981), Theater Row, New York.*

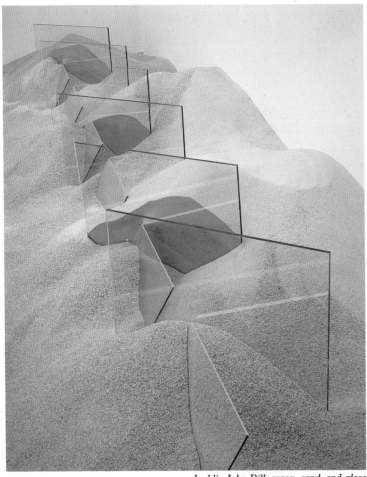

*Laddie John Dill: argon, sand, and glass
environment (1971, courtesy of the artist).*
Photo by © Susan Einstein

Laddie John Dill was drawn to neon by its "vibrancy of color." For him, neon was a stepping stone: he created a series of temporary neon environments in 1970-73 that led on to permanent works of cement and glass. In some of these early works, neon and argon tubes were laid out on an undulating "landscape" of reflective silica sand; in others, argon tubes were buried, and the light was channeled out through the plates of glass set at angles in the sand above the tubes. In both, there was a subtle interplay of direct and diffused light, and a dramatic juxtaposition of solid/liquid and transparent/opaque. Dill also made a series of segmented tubes, filled with argon or helium, each segment of which was a different shade of white or clear glass. The gas glowed in a series of variations on its natural hue.

Dill has occasionally returned to his neon and sand environments—for the 1981 WPA show in Washington, D.C. and, most recently, as the set for a production of Benjamin Britten's opera *Death in Venice* at the Long Beach Civic Auditorium. Behind the performance area, sixteen stepped-up furrows of sand glowed softly beneath a vividly painted backdrop. The artist also plans to incorporate neon into relief compositions of glass and painted canvas. Dill works in Venice, California.

Laddie John Dill: detail of model for
Death in Venice *opera set (1983, courtesy
the artist)*

Michael Hayden, a Canadian artist who recently moved to Los Angeles, has been described as a "poet in sculpted light." He dropped out of architecture school, and taught himself chemistry, computer technology, and the properties of gas, skills he has deployed in an impressive series of works for private collectors and public buildings.

He has developed a palette of seventy-two durable colors for his tubes. He uses miniaturized transformers and high-frequency charges in order to eliminate the clutter of wires and electrodes. Many of his pieces are animated by microprocessors, using sophisticated computer programs. His most spectacular achievement is the 570-foot-long *L'Arc en Ciel* (1978) that is integrated into the glass atrium of a Toronto subway station. It is computer-animated and activated by heat sensors to indicate approaching trains. At night it serves as a beacon for passing cars and planes. For passengers on the concourse below, it is like looking up at the stained glass of a cathedral. A smaller, jazzier version of this idea roofs a pedestrian walkway in downtown Los Angeles. Hayden has also brought his rainbows indoors, enclosing them in polycarbonate tubes and suspending them from loops of clear plastic.

Michael Hayden: Lumetric Pummel *(1980, collection of Mr. and Mrs. Rudge Allen, Houston).* Photo by © Rudge Allen

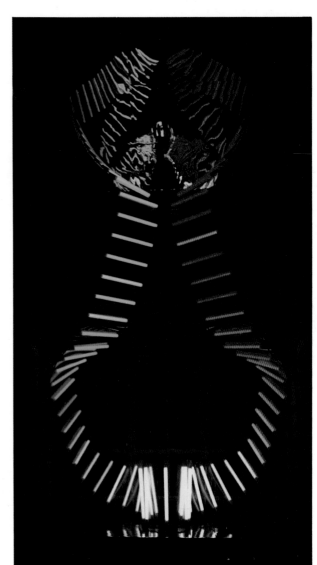

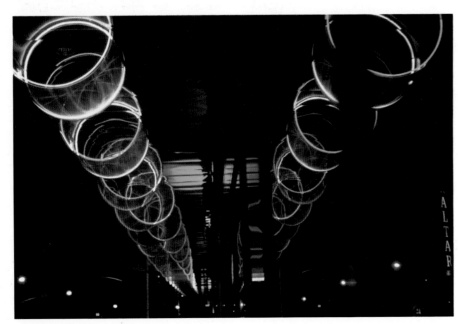

Michael Hayden: Generators of the Cylinder *(1982, International Jewelery Center), Los Angeles.* Photo by © Kristina Lucas

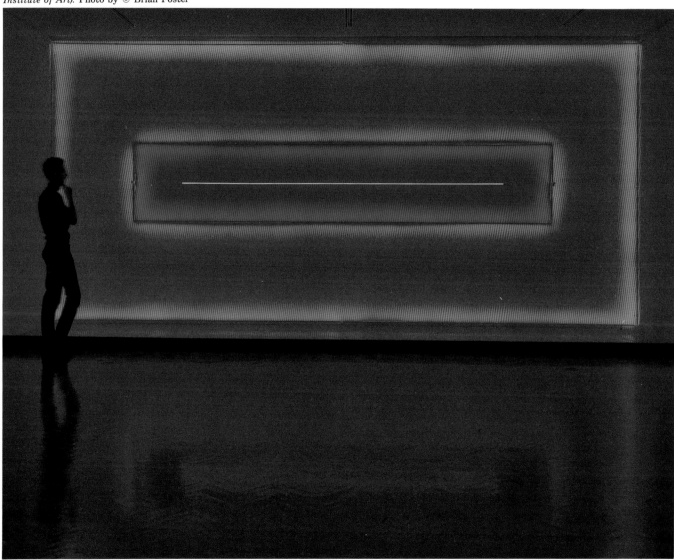

Cork Marcheschi: Experience at Council Grove *(1982, collection of Minneapolis Institute of Art).* Photo by © Brian Foster

Cork Marcheschi is part poet, part electronics buff. For the past twelve years, he has worked and taught in Minneapolis, but he grew up in the Bay Area in the fifties, and retains an affection for the beat era. As a kid, he created a "Casa Loco" in the basement, conducting endless experiments with electronic castoffs. "Electricity is a material that can be manipulated," he remarks. "The mysteries of light and life are very close, and I enjoy dealing with a material that is and isn't there." Critic Melinda Wortz wrote, "Marcheschi has the sensibility of a folk artist, whose materials are found energy and found objects. His romantic, virtuoso installations. . . are as awesome as a science fiction movie."

She was describing the work that Marcheschi created in the first ten years of his career, beginning in 1967. These kinetic, viewer-activated sculptures, featuring flashing lights, crackling arcs of electricity and a whiff of Dr. Frankenstein's laboratory, belong to the third of our categories. Many, indeed, make no use of neon. But, since 1977, Marcheschi has been creating color field paintings with neon: haloed squares and rectangles that recall the canvases of Mark Rothko. He superimposes two tubes, masks them with opaque latex paint, then scores a line on the rear of each, allowing the light to project back onto the wall, creating inner and outer penumbras of complementary colors. The technique is not immediately evident, and, even when you see how it is done, you are still entranced by the effect.

William Shipman: Vanity; *neon, fiberglass,
and polyester resin (1981, courtesy
the artist).* Photo by © Glenn Eddins

The WPA show offered Marcheschi a challenging site: the windows of the old Willard Hotel, around the corner from the Washington Momument and Pennsylvania Avenue. A display of neon so close to hallowed ground might have provoked controversy. But Marcheschi's *Green Doors* justified their prominence with serene assurance, drawing passersby like moths to the flame. He has also created large-scale neon sculptures in Minneapolis and Seattle, and a roomsized version of his neon projections.

Marcheschi helped inspire *William Shipman* in Kansas City to switch from paint to neon. Like his mentor, Shipman is a scavenger of objects—notably old neon signs—that provide him with inspiration or materials for his art. But the closest parallel is with another of Shipman's heroes: the Italian plasterer Simon Rodia, who transformed junk into a fantastic group of towers in the Watts district of Los Angeles. Shipman trained as an artist and works as a mechanic. The pure, intense colors of neon lured him away from painting, and he developed (by trial and error) an idiosyncratic way of using it.

He describes a figure he made from salvaged neon signs: "an ice cream cone formed the body, a letter P the head, a B (from a beer sign) the breasts, and a pair of Dairycream arrows the nipples." These constructions—some figurative, some not—are enclosed within and supported by a translucent membrane of fiberglass and polyester resin. "Think of the neon as bones, the membrane as skin," he suggests. "Electricity infuses the composition with energy, but, even when it is off, there's the sculptural form." Shipman's work is rooted in a sense of place: "my work is not pretty, it expresses the anxiety of the ghetto."

Two California artists, *Victoria Rivers* and *William Kane*, have recently begun to use neon as a means of energizing textured surfaces, achieving a beguiling sensuality. Kentucky-born Rivers has integrated painted tubes within her seductive compositions of hand-dyed and printed fabrics. The light suffuses the silks, velvets, and ribbons, accentuating the colors, patterns, and textures. Rivers works in Sacramento.

Kane is an accomplished photographer, who turned from natural to urban landscapes, making stark black-and-white blowups of decrepit city walls. He first used neon in 1978 as an incandescent extension of the graffiti in his images. One of these photomurals was displayed high above the streets of San Francisco (where Kane works) in a 1979 billboard exhibition. For the WPA exhibition, he applied a bold neon scrawl to a real wall, creating an eerie green glow within the darkened parking lot.

Both Kane and Rivers use neon to achieve a dramatic contrast between line and plane, smooth and rough, light-giving and light-receiving.

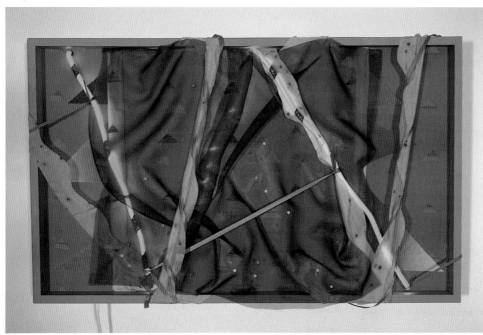

Victoria Rivers: Birthday Party *(1981, courtesy the artist).* Photo by Donald Satterlee

Victoria Rivers: Daggers *(1982, courtesy the artist).* Photo by Donald Satterlee

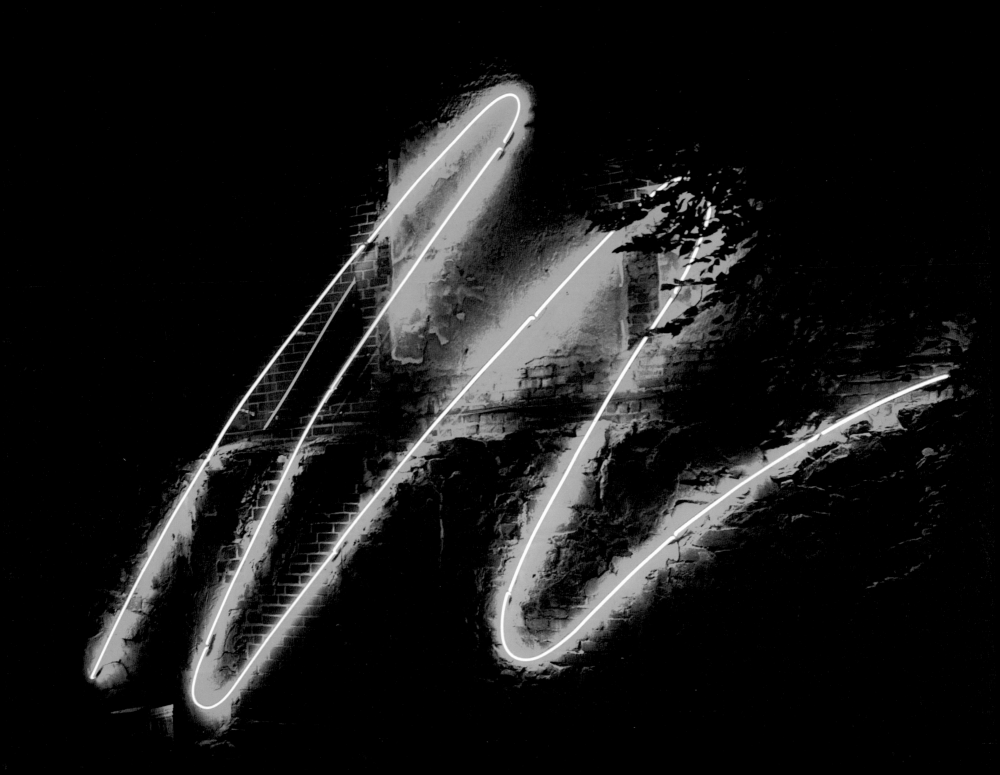

William Kane: Untitled *(1981, Neon Fronts exhibition, Washington, DC)*

Dale Chihuly and James Carpenter: Neon Environment *(1972, Rhode Island School of Design).* Courtesy Dale Chihuly

73

Paul Seide learned his craft as the next-to-last graduate of the Egani Institute (for neon tube bending) in New York, which closed its doors in 1971. He continued his education at the Rhode Island School of Design under the direction of Dale Chihuly, an acclaimed teacher and glass artist. Working with a former pupil, James Carpenter, Chihuly had created a series of glass and neon environments in the early seventies. Their fantastic imagery and sophisticated technology was a major influence on Seide when he established his own studio in New York in 1978.

For Seide, "... electrically charged gas is like the genie in the bottle. It's possible to create color—to cause light to vibrate at the frequency of red, for example." Using an oscillator to generate high-frequency radio waves, he can activate gas even through very thick pieces of glass. He has also experimented with different kinds of fluorescent glass, and has introduced rare earth colorants into ordinary soda lime glass. His work has evolved from loops mounted atop a transformer, to seductive jewels of colored glass that have no need of electrodes.

Even so incomplete a chronicle of artists utilizing neon for its light and color must include mention of *Dan Flavin.* Flavin uses standard fluorescent tubes rather than neon, arranging them in austere constructions that suffuse rooms or public spaces with intense color. In addition to his many gallery exhibits, he also has created light sculptures—over the tracks of New York's Grand Central Station, and in the Hauserman showroom at the Pacific Design Center in West Hollywood.

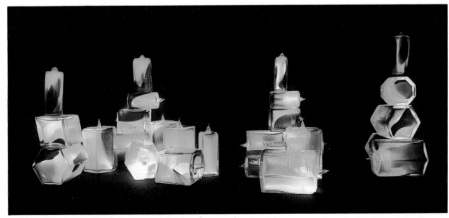

Paul Seide: Tucson Tableau *(1983, collection of Tucson Museum of Art), Arizona.* Photo by © John Baldwin

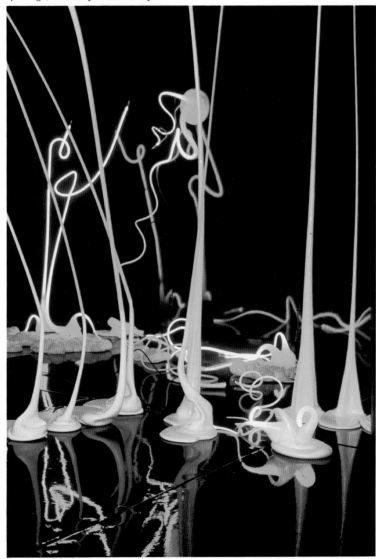

Kinetic and Performance Art

Keith Sonnier regards the viewer as a participant in his work. Beginning in 1969, he developed a series he entitled *BA-O-BA* (a Haitian word that signifies a body bathed in light or color). His choice of image may derive from childhood memories of rural Louisiana, where distant neon signs created an unearthly glow across the rice fields. As an artist in New York (and on frequent trips to Europe) his means were less pastoral: a sheet of glass reflected the person bathed in neon light; a video camera transmitted a picture of the interaction. Thus the viewer became as much a part of the composition as the exposed wires and transformer: the art served as a performance area.

Early *BA-O-BA* pieces arranged a few straight and curved tubes in a manner that suggested a human face; later examples substituted enameled panels for the glass, and a Mondrian-like geometry of tubing. In 1978, Sonnier introduced a new series, *SEL*, that were inspired by examples of early Chinese calligraphy he had seen on a visit to that country. The *SEL* pieces were tighter and more formal; more to be admired as works of art than actively to engage the viewer.

Lee Champagne (of Benicia, California) studied art and theology, and he uses Catholic iconography as a framework for social satire. His major work to date, *Chapel Champagne, Shrine of Latter Day Neon Nuanced Naivete*, was completed in 1982. It comprises separate pieces, arranged as in a chapel, with altar, prayer stool, and side reliquaries. But the altar resembles a juke box, the reliquaries are coin-operated, and kneeling on the stool activates a video monitor and a recording of Gregorian chant. Champagne uses neon as a metaphor: in its guises as a selling medium and as a light to dispel ignorance and darkness. Neon supplies the seductive hues to augment richly painted and ornamented assemblages. One of these, entitled *St. Farrah Ferrari's Fast Food Fantasty* (1980), incorporates McDonalds' golden arches within a Gothic diptych.

Larry Albright cheerfully admits to

Keith Sonnier: Sel I*(1978, courtesy the artist).* Photo courtesy Keith Sonnier

Larry Albright: krypton-filled sphere (1982, courtesy the artist)

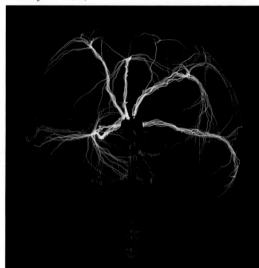

the role of mad scientist. Working in a cluttered studio behind his home in Venice, California, he creates beautiful, but dangerous-looking spherical light shows. He fills glass spheres, twelve to eighteen inches in diameter, with krypton or other rare gases. He charges the gas with 5,000 up to 80,000 volts, creating an escalation of effects: lazy swirls of light, tremulous tentacles, and violent explosions of energy whose pattern can be changed by touching the surface of the glass.

Albright bought a neon shop in order to learn the technique, and today he is as much in demand as a technical wizard as an artist. One of his spheres was featured in an otherwise forgettable movie, *Battle Beyond the Stars,* in which a slanty-eyed alien described it as: "a stellar converter, the most dangerous weapon in the universe." In an earlier work, Albright filled a tangle of tubes with a mixture of neon and mercury. As the tubes warmed up, the mercury vaporized, pushing back the neon and creating a two-way surge of red and black.

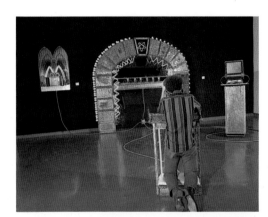

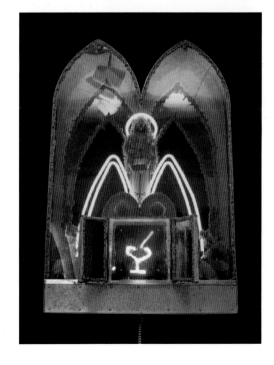

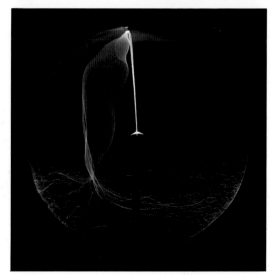

Lee Champagne: St. Farrah Ferrari's Fast Food Fantasy *(1980, courtesy the artist).*
Courtesy Lee Champagne

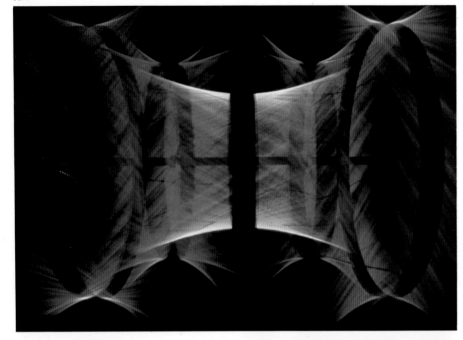

Alejandro Sina: Spinning Shaft *(1981,
courtesy the artist).* Photo © by Alejandro Sina

76

Alejandro Sina grew up in Chile, came to MIT on a Fulbright scholarship in 1973, and worked there as a research fellow through 1979. Subsequently, he stayed on in Boston, working independently with Otto Piene at MIT's Center for Advanced Visual Studies. Like Albright, Sina creates electrically charged globes, but his are immersed in water tanks, which cause a spectacular glow when you touch the glass. He suspends single-electrode tubes like mobiles: within a building, from helium balloons arching over New York's Central Park, and, even more ambitiously, as a 500-foot tail to a kite that is to be flown over Tokyo, and as a 350-foot-long sculpture over the tracks of the Harvard subway station.

His electro-mechanical pieces dazzle the eye. He developed the concept after looking at time-exposure photographs of the hanging pieces, which move gently in air currents. The motorized tubes—unimpressive at rest—create cyclones of colored light, their edges fraying like strands of silk, or the illusion of a butterfly fluttering atop a flexible rod. Sina plans to install a trio of spinning propellers at Boston's Logan Airport.

Several artists have used neon in performance art and in combination with natural elements. *Christian Schiess,* a former physical anthropologist based in San Francisco, is one of the most eclectic. He is attracted to the concept of the ancient alchemists, that the world is composed of four elements: fire, water, earth, and air. He has submerged neon under a lake, threaded it through a grassy meadow, and suspended it in inflated vinyl bags. Schiess has also devised neon costumes for dancers, and has captured the Chinese ribbon effect on film.

Neon has figured prominently in the work of photo-realist painters. *Robert Cottingham* travels across America by bus, documenting old signs and peeling facades with his Hasselblad. Back in his Connecticut studio, he transmutes these images into sharp-eyed visions of the urban landscape that have something of Edward Hopper's eye for the telling detail.

For Cottingham, photographs are a point of departure, the material for his art. For *William Christenberry,* a Washington, D.C. artist, old signs (painted and neon) are a link to his roots in rural Alabama. He collects them for

Christian Schiess: light suit from film
Lumens *(1980, courtesy the artist).*
Courtesy Christian Schiess

Robert Cottingham: The Spot; *acrylic on paper,
derived from photograph of old sign, (1978,
courtesy the artist).* Photo by ©
D. James Dee

Right: *Red Goose Shoes sign found by William Christenberry in Memphis, 1967.* Photo by © William Christenberry

Far right: *William Christenberry,* Untitled; *neon and wood (1971, courtesy the artist).* Photo by © William Christenberry

their beauty as found objects, and to incorporate them—directly or indirectly—in his photographs and sculptures. Around 1970, he installed small pieces of neon in polished wood cases (both found objects), and threaded tubes through boxes and wooden rods, achieving both a shock effect and a surprising harmony of natural and man-made materials.

For *Robert Rauschenberg,* photographs of old signs are an end in themselves, the chronicle of an idiosyncratic attitude towards the medium. To accompany the photographs shown here, he wrote: "I know the excuse or use of neon is mainly to carry information after dark, but I am reminded of a statement made a few years back by Princess Vicky Alliata claiming that most women don't have sense enough to wear their lame while the sun is shining. Within the same consciousness the necessary physical characteristics of neon, including the rigidity and fragility of the materials and the tolerance of hostile attack of weather produce some of the most unique drawing in art. I like my neon on, in sunshine, blanching all of the gross colors and providing a network of changing lines, shadows and hardware."

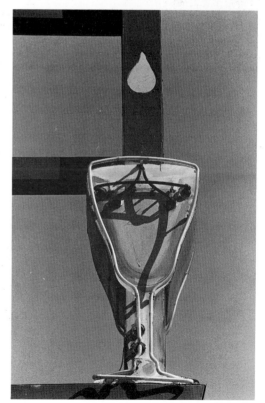

Old neon signs, photographed by Robert Rauschenberg © (Untitled Press)

Neon Outdoors

Jerry Noe: Neon Pond *(1970). Noe, an artist who teaches at the University of North Carolina, Chapel Hill, uses neon in juxtaposition with natural and man-made objects, and by itself as softly flowing lines of pure light. Courtesy Jerry Noe*

Fred Escher: Neon sculpture in 9 Artists, 9 Spaces *outdoor exhibition (1970), St. Paul, Minnesota. Escher is now a painter in New York. Courtesy Fred Escher*

Fred Tschida: Light in Movement, 7, *neon on car crossing Bonneville Salt Flats, Utah (1980). Tschida teaches glass design at Alfred University, New York, and uses neon in transient events that are documented in photographs.* **Photo by** © Eliza Tonachel

Eric Zimmerman: LA 200th *(1981), a birthday cake for Los Angeles's Bicentennial, originally designed as a rooftop inflatable. Zimmerman is a Los Angeles artist who creates computer-programed, mirror-boxed neons and neon lighting for his father's architectural practice.*

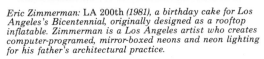

John David Mooney: Doll's House for Lady Di, *commissioned by* Architectural Design *magazine for a London exhibition of architect-designed doll houses to celebrate the birth of Prince William. Mooney, a Chicago artist, has created temporary environments up to several miles long, and large light sculptures in Chicago and Los Angeles.* Courtesy John David Mooney

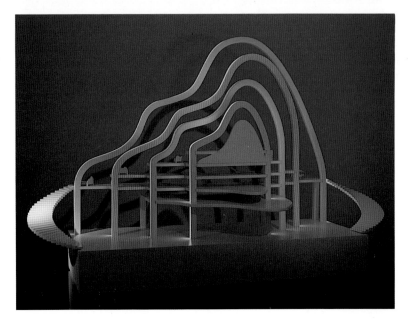

Bibliography

Baker, Elizabeth. "The Light Brigade." *Art News,* March 1967.

Georgia, Olivia. *Neon Fronts.* Catalog of WPA exhibition, Washington, DC, 1983.

Kepes, Gyorgy. "Light and Design." *Design Quarterly* 68, Walker Art Center, Minneapolis, 1967.

Light, Motion, Space. Catalog of exhibition at Walker Art Center, Minneapolis, 1967.

Lighting Dimensions. 31706 S. Coast Highway, Suite 302, South Laguna, CA 92677. Monthly.

Mack, Kathy. *American Neon.* New York: Universe Books, 1976.

Miller, Samuel. *Neon Techniques and Handling: Handbook of Neon Signs and Cold Cathode Lighting.* Third Edition. Cincinnati: Signs of the Times Publishing, 1977.

Piene, Nan. "Light Art." *Art in America,* May-June 1967.

Proux, Michel. *Electric Art.* New York: Rizzoli International, 1977.

Restanay, Pierre. *Chryssa.* New York: Abrams, 1977.

Richardson, Brenda. *Bruce Nauman: Neons.* Catalog of exhibition at Baltimore Museum of Art, 1982.

Rosenzweig, Solomon and Maureen Brierton. "Light as Art: A Historical Perspective." *Designers West,* October 1981.

Schwartz, Rolf. *Neon.* Dortmund, Germany: Harenberg, 1980.

Shapiro, David. *Stephen Antonakos: New Works.* Catalog of exhibition at Roslyn Harbor, NY: Nassau County Museum of Fine Arts, 1982.

Signs of the Times. 407 Gilbert Avenue, Cincinnati, OH 45202. Monthly. (Special features on neon in March, December 1981.)

Stern, Rudi. *Let There Be Neon.* New York: Abrams, 1979.

Stone, Jill. *Times Square: A Pictorial History.* New York: Collier, 1982.

Transformer. Museum of Neon Art, 704 Traction Avenue, Los Angeles CA 90013. Quarterly.

Venturi, Robert, Denise Scott Brown, Steven Izenour. *Learning from Las Vegas.* Second Edition. Cambridge: MIT Press, 1979.

Wolfe, Tom. "Electrographic Architecture." *Architectural Design,* London, July 1969.

Wolfe, Tom. *Kandy-Kolored Tangerine-Flake Streamline Baby.* New York: Farrah, Strauss Giroux, 1965.

Wortz, Melinda. *Cork Marcheschi: Experience at Council Grove.* Catalog of exhibition at Minneapolis Institute of Arts, 1982.

Classes in Neon Fabrication and/or Design

The Egani Institute in New York, which closed in 1971, was once *the* place to learn the craft of neon. It is estimated that 80 per cent of glass benders learned their skills there. Instruction focussed entirely on technique; artistry was rigorously excluded. The Institute's sole aim was to turn out proficient signmakers. Nothing reflects the new awareness of neon's potential better than the proliferation of workshops and university courses that offer instruction both in aesthetics and the technique of glass bending. They include:

California.

California Neon Workshop: Floyd Le Brun teaches an intensive six-week course. Fee: $3000. P.O. Box 1356, Antioch 94509. Tel. (415) 778-3500

Museum of Neon Art: Lili Lakich and Richard Jenkins, 704 Traction Ave., LA 90013. Tel. (213) 617-1580 (Courses for beginners and intermediate students are offered through UCLA Extension; student designs are sent out to be fabricated. Course fee: $135, plus materials)

Academy of Art College, Fine Art Dept., 40 Powell Street, San Francisco 94108. Tel. (415) 673-4200 (Christian Schiess teaches beginners' and advanced courses in neon sculpture, utilising a fully equipped workshop. Fee: $480 for undergraduate credit course)

Illinois.

Lightwriters Neon: Jacob Fishman, Box 22 HW, Winnetka 60093. Tel. (312) 441-9115 (Introductory and intensive courses, and personal instruction, in design and fabrication. Fee for 30-hour introductory course: $360)

Minnesota.

Minneapolis College of Art and Design, 133 E. 25th Street, Minneapolis 55404. Tel. (612) 870-3346 (Cork Marcheschi teaches ten-week extension classes. Course fee: $140, plus materials.)

North Carolina.

University of North Carolina, Art Dept., 115 S. Columbia Street, Chapel Hill 27514. Tel. (919) 962-2015 (Jerry Noe teaches occasional courses on neon as an art medium.)

New York.

New York Experimental Glass Works, 142 Mulberry Street, NY 10013. Tel. (212) 966-1808 (Established in 1977 to further the appreciation and utilization of glass as an artistic medium. Professional artists administer a wide range of programs, including introductory and intermediate hands-on neon courses, which are available for credit through Parsons and the New School. Instructors include Joseph Upham, David Ablon, Bill Gudenrath and Gaper Ingui. Course fees: $300-350)

Washington.

City Art Works, 1902 Main Street, Seattle 98144. Tel. (206) 625-4572 (James Morris supervises an introductory course in tube bending, in addition to individual instruction. Course fee: $125, plus supplies)

Wisconsin.

Northern Wisconsin Neon Workshop, Box 92, Antigo 54409. Tel. (715) 623-3000 (Dean Blazek teaches an intensive six-week course that, like Egani, is designed to produce glass benders who will take jobs in the industry. Course fee: $3000 for 240 hours of instruction. Each course has a maximum of five students and is oversubscribed.)

Neon Workshops

Most of these workshops have been established in the last few years by a craftsperson, working with one or two assistants, to create custom designs (signs, decorative pieces, lighting) and collectibles.

California.

Archigraphics: Eric Zimmerman, 3025 Exposition Place, Los Angeles 90018. Tel. (213) 291-8089

Custom Neon: Charles di Bona, 3804 Beverly Blvd., Los Angeles 90004. Tel. (213) 386-7945

Neon Neon: Karen Heisler and Joanne Crawford, 3692 17th Street, San Francisco 94114. Tel. (415) 552-4163

Illinois.

Neonics Chicago: Richard Warrum, 3906 N. Broadway, Chicago 60613. Tel. (312) 472-7444 (Manufacturing and commercial sales. For retail and custom design, the address is: Light & Space Design, 3324 N. Halsted, Chicago 60657)

Lightwriters Neon (see Classes in Neon)

Indiana.

The Village Neon Shoppe: Steve Renner, 305 York Road, Yorktown 47396. Tel. (317) 759-9133

Michigan.

Planet Neon: Jeffrey Heyn, P.O. Box 284, 46593 Grand River, Novi 48050. Tel. (313) 348-8150

Minnesota.

B. Jirka & Associates, 16 W. 35th Street, Minneapolis 55408. Tel. (612) 822-9000

Missouri.

Magick Signs: Ronald Overby, 122 West Fifth Street, Kansas City 64105. Tel. (816) 221-1518

Montana.

Alliance Neon, 238 Anderson Drive, P.O. Box 1119, Helena 59624. Tel. (406) 443-4309

New York.

Design Circuit International: Robert Lobi, 141 Fifth Avenue, NY 10010. Tel. (212) 533-9630 (Specializing in design and technology for discos and other interior lighting)

Let There Be Neon: Rudi Stern, 451 W. Broadway, NY 10012. Tel. (212) 473-8630 (Versatile workshop, headed by one of the pioneers of the neon revival)

Neon New York: Michael Hauenstein, 55 Bethune Street, NY 10014. Tel. (212) 242-3585 (Custom design and fabrication, principally for interiors)

Say It In Neon: Pacifico Palumbo, 434 Hudson Street, NY 10014. Tel. (212) 691-7977 (Unusual collectibles and custom design)

Texas.

Dr. Neon: Tim Reardon, 6721 N. Lamar Blvd. Austin 78752. Tel. (512) 451-1117

Sculptured Neon Company: Greg Garnett, 4078 Hampshire, Fort Worth 76103. Tel. (817) 534-8445

Washington.

Jimmy Neon: James Morris, 1116 McKenzie, Bremerton 98310. Tel. (206) 479-6636

Washington, DC

Neon Projects: Ted Bonar and Larry Kanter, 2424 18th Street NW, DC 20009. Tel. (202) 797-8722 (Fabricated many of the art works in the 1981 WPA exhibition, "Neon Fronts")

Neon Sign Companies

A few of the larger companies. For a full listing, check local Yellow Pages.

California.

American Neon and Graphics, 11260 Sherman Way, Sun Valley 91352. Tel. (213) 875-1815 (Unique among the large companies in its exclusive emphasis on neon. Specializes in large-scale projects for the entertainment industry)

Illinois.

Mount Vernon Neon Sign Company, Salem Road and Park Avenue, P.O. Box 1007, Mount Vernon 62864. Tel. (618) 242-0645

Maryland.

Claude Neon Signs, 1808 Cherry Hill Rd., Baltimore 21230. Tel. (301) 685-7575

New York.

Artkraft-Strauss Sign Company, 830 12th Avenue, New York 10019. Tel. (212) 265-5155

Midtown Neon Sign Company, 550 W. 30th Street, New York 10001. Tel. (212) 736-3838

Universal Electric Sign Company, 59-26 55th Drive, Maspeth 11378. Tel. (212) 894-4800

Pennsylvania.

Greater Pittsburgh Neon, 5102 Butler Street, Pittsburgh 15201. Tel. (412) 782-6366

Texas.

Houston Neon Fabricators, 6102-C Milwee, Houston 77092. Tel. (713) 957-8718

Texas Neon Advertising Company, 245 W. Josephine, San Antonio 78212. Tel. (512) 734-6694

Utah.

Young Electric Sign Company, 336 S. 400 W., Salt Lake City 84110. Tel. (801) 363-8900 (Branches in Las Vegas and 11 other western cities)

Wisconsin.

Everbrite Electric Signs, 315 Marion Avenue, Milwaukee 53211. Tel. (414) 762-8700

Neon Preservation and Collectors

California.

Museum of Neon Art: Lili Lakich, 704 Traction Avenue, Los Angeles 90013. Tel. (213) 617-1580 (MoNA opened in April 1982 as the first museum devoted to the exhibition, documentation and preservation of neon, electric and kinetic art. MoNA is seeking donations of exceptional signs and art works. It encourages restoration, and is currently trying to relocate the 25-foot-high jitterbugging couple created for the premiere of *Zoot Suit.*)

Save Our Neon Organization: Gloria Poore, Grade, 701 Island Avenue, San Diego 92101 (SONO was established in 1980 by three artists to preserve, restore and recycle San Diego's rich heritage of neon. Signs and movie marquees, including the Campus Drive-In, are currently in storage, awaiting a good home.)

Indiana.

Nostalgic Neon: Steve Renner, 305 York Road, Yorktown 47396. Tel. (317) 759-9133 (Renner has a large collection of neon clocks and is beginning a collectors' association.)

Ohio.

Tod Swormstedt, 2825 Rosella Avenue, Cincinnati 45208 (Swormstedt, editor of *Signs of the Times*, publishes a newsletter directed towards other collectors of neon beer signs.)

Pennsylvania.

Leonard Davidson, 860 N. 26th Street, Philadelphia 19130 (Davidson has a major collection of classic signs.)

Photograph by Mary Jane O'Donnell

Michael Webb is a writer and photographer of architecture and design. He is the curator and major contributor to a Smithsonian Institution traveling exhibition, also entitled "The Magic of Neon," and plans to produce a documentary film on the subject. He has conducted a seminar on neon at the University of California in Los Angeles.

Webb is author of *Architecture in Britain Today* (Paul Hamlyn, 1968) and is contributing editor on *Arts and Architecture* magazine. His articles and photographs have also been published in *Architectural Digest, Design Quarterly, Historic Preservation, Portfolio,* and other leading magazines.

His other major interest is film. The former Director of National Film Programing for The American Film Institute, he has more recently scripted and produced films for the Smithsonian and commercial television. He is currently developing another traveling exhibition for the Smithsonian, *Hollywood: Legend and Reality.*

Michael Webb was born in London, and worked there as a correspondent for the *Times* and as an associate editor for *Country Life.* He moved to the United States in 1969 and now lives in Los Angeles.